AMAZING FEATS OF

ENVIRONMENTAL ENGINEERING

Essential Library

An Imprint of Abdo Publishing | www.abdopublishing.com

ENVIRONMENTAL ENGINEERING

by Carol Hand

Content Consultant

James H. Clarke, PhD, BCES, F. AAFS
Professor of the Practice of Civil and Environmental Engineering
Professor of Earth and Environmental Sciences
Director of Graduate Studies for Environmental Engineering
Vanderbilt University

www.abdopublishing.com

Published by Abdo Publishing, a division of ABDO, PO Box 398166, Minneapolis, Minnesota 55439. Copyright © 2015 by Abdo Consulting Group, Inc. International copyrights reserved in all countries. No part of this book may be reproduced in any form without written permission from the publisher. Essential Library™ is a trademark and logo of Abdo Publishing.

Printed in the United States of America, North Mankato, Minnesota
042014
092014

THIS BOOK CONTAINS
RECYCLED MATERIALS

Cover Photo: Ted S. Warren/AP Images
Interior Photos: Ted S. Warren/AP Images, 2; Gerald Herbert/AP Images, 7; Patrick Semansky/AP Images, 10, 31, 37; badmanproduction/Thinkstock, 15; Goodluz/Thinkstock, 17; Lynn Johnson/Corbis, 22; Adam Woolfitt/Corbis, 25; Dave Martin/AP Images, 27; amiralio/Thinkstock, 41; RTSubin/Thinkstock, 44; Martchan/Shutterstock Images, 47; NinaMalyna/Thinkstock, 51; Jerome Delay/AP Images, 55; Goran Bogicevic/Shutterstock Images, 57; Red Line Editorial, 62; DutchlightNetherlands/Thinkstock, 67; AP Images, 70; ChrisDoDutch/Thinkstock, 73; M-Sat Ltd/Science Source, 77; avillaschi/Thinkstock, 80; Carlos Barria/Reuters Pool/AP Images, 83; Senseo Coffee System/PRNewsFoto/AP Images, 85; Ron Chapple Stock/Thinkstock, 87; James S. Tyree/AP Images, 89; Peter Essick/Corbis, 93

Editor: Amanda Lanser
Series Designer: Becky Daum

Library of Congress Control Number: 2014932584

Cataloging-in-Publication Data

Hand, Carol.
  Amazing feats of environmental engineering / Carol Hand.
    p. cm. -- (Great achievements in engineering)
  Includes index.
  ISBN 978-1-62403-429-9
  1. Environmental engineering--Juvenile literature.   I. Title.
  628--dc23

                                2014932584

Cover: A Superfund project manager inspects water from a contaminated source before and after treatment.

CONTENTS

CHAPTER 1

A SPILL IN THE GULF

At 9:49 on the evening of April 20, 2010, a massive explosion rocked the oil-drilling rig *Deepwater Horizon* in the Gulf of Mexico. Another explosion followed ten seconds later. Flames engulfed the rig, and 11 men were killed instantly. Pandemonium followed. The remaining 115 people scrambled for lifeboats. Ten of them, trying desperately to avoid the inferno, threw themselves off the rig floor into the water approximately 100 feet (31 m) below. The worst oil spill disaster in US history, and the second largest in the world, had begun.

Fire rages on the *Deepwater Horizon* a day after explosions rocked the oil rig.

The US Department of the Interior did not require BP to write a detailed environmental analysis of the *Deepwater Horizon*. BP's official Regional Spill Plan for the Gulf, approved by the Department of the Interior in 2009, described a need to protect walruses, an Arctic animal not found in the waters of the Gulf of Mexico. It listed a wildlife expert who had died four years previously, and gave a Japanese home-shopping website as an equipment supplier. Part of the plan was written in pencil. Just one of 600 pages in the plan concerned stopping an oil leak. After the 2010 *Deepwater Horizon* spill, the misinformation and errors in BP's plan led many people to believe the company was unprepared for an oil spill in the Gulf of Mexico.

The Macondo oil well is owned by BP, a company originally named British Petroleum. BP had leased the drilling rig from Transocean, the world's largest deepwater driller. The rig sat above more than 5,000 feet (1,520 m) of water, and a pipe extended down through another 13,360 feet (4,072 m) of earth into the well.[1] Gas had rushed up the pipe from the oil well into the rig and exploded.

Two days after the explosions, the pipe connecting the *Deepwater Horizon* to the Macondo oil well snapped as the rig toppled into the Gulf of Mexico. Oil gushed into the deep waters of the Gulf. Oil flowed at a rate of 55,800 to 68,200 barrels per day until June 3, when the pipe was finally cut. Even then, oil continued to flow at a slightly lower rate, between 47,700 and 58,300 barrels per day, until workers finally capped the pipe on July 15—nearly three months after the spill began.[2]

WHY DO BLOWOUTS HAPPEN?

Blowouts on oil rigs are huge, concentrated spills with devastating consequences. Even a well-engineered drilling rig is a dangerous place. Petroleum trapped in the bedrock is under extremely high pressure, and the deeper the well is, the higher the pressure is. This petroleum is always ready to blow, and drilling into it is a treacherous business. It is common for rigs to have trouble keeping the pressure under control. When drillers completely lose control of the pressure, a blowout occurs, and oil and gas explode up and out through the pipe. The *Deepwater Horizon* had a blowout preventer (BOP), a mechanism designed to close off the pipe in the event of a blowout, but it had failed. Blowouts are expected to be increasingly frequent as companies drill wells deeper and deeper under the world's oceans.

When the worst happens and a blowout occurs, the ocean is soon awash with millions of gallons of thick, sticky, toxic oil that coats and poisons sea animals, covers hundreds of miles of coastline beaches,

and damages people's health and destroys their livelihoods. Managing the cleanup of this gooey mess becomes the responsibility of environmental engineers and scientists.

DEEPWATER HORIZON CLEANUP

The massive *Deepwater Horizon* cleanup involved not only BP but also many federal and state agencies. Early cleanup efforts included four technologies commonly used in oil spills: controlled burns, chemical dispersants, booms to corral the oil, and skimmers. After the initial oil slicks were removed, manual cleanup continued as oil washed into shallow waters and onto beaches in five states.

The *Deepwater Horizon*'s blowout preventer failed to close off the pipe, allowing oil to spill into the ocean.

BLOWOUT PREVENTER FAILURE

The pipe running from the *Deepwater Horizon* passed through a channel in the Macondo's 40-foot (12 m) BOP before entering the well. The BOP's structure included a series of valves and a series of scissorlike structures. During a blowout, these safeguards should cut through the channel, crush the pipe, and seal off the flow of oil. But the Macondo's BOP failed.

An investigation after the spill showed the BOP's battery was dead. A coil in a piece of equipment controlling the valves was wired in reverse, preventing them from closing. Finally, the pipe inside the BOP was stuck at a strange angle so it could not be closed off. All of these flaws contributed to the spill in April 2010.

In June 2013, BP announced the US Coast Guard was ending its cleanup efforts along the coasts of Mississippi, Alabama, and Florida. But even three years after the incident, the cleanup was far from complete. Coastal sediments still contained oil, and cleanup continued along approximately 165 miles (266 km) of Louisiana shoreline. Crews were still finding oil and lumps of solidified oil called tar balls there. Workers in the seafood industry, particularly crab and oyster fishermen, still had not recovered economically. They predicted their catch would be depleted for at least another five years.

CLEANING OIL-SOAKED BIRDS

Cleaning an oil-soaked bird is a low-tech, hands-on process. First, the bird is warmed. It is fed up to eight times a day for as many as five days and often rehydrated through a feeding tube. The rehydrating process flushes out toxic oil from the bird's system. Then two people wash the bird in water that contains a small amount of Dawn detergent using hands, toothbrushes, and cotton swabs. A Waterpik, commonly used to clean human teeth, is used to clean around the bird's eyes. The people cleaning the bird must change the water frequently. For example, it can take up to 300 gallons (1,100 L) of water to wash a single pelican. After washing it, the workers rinse the bird carefully with a spa nozzle. Then, the bird sits under a pet dryer and preens its feathers until they are aligned properly. Finally, it recuperates in an outdoor pool for several days, though it may be months before it is released. In the year after the oil spill, volunteers cleaned and released 1,252 birds.[3]

FUTURE ENVIRONMENTAL ENGINEERING CHALLENGES

Perhaps the biggest lesson from the *Deepwater Horizon* disaster is that a new and creative generation of environmental engineers is needed to deal with future oil spills. But cleaning up oil spills is just one of many career avenues a future environmental engineer might take. Engineers and scientists are involved at every step of the oil drilling process, from locating the oil to building and operating the rig. But they are also needed in other industries. In 2002, the United Nations (UN) Environment Programme created a list of environmental issues the global community will experience in the coming century. All these issues will challenge future environmental engineers.

In this century, the most significant environmental problem facing the world community will likely be global climate change. As increasing energy use leads to the emission of greenhouse gases including carbon dioxide into the atmosphere, Earth's climate is warming and climatic activity is becoming more extreme. Coastal areas are beginning to flood and suffer damaging storms. Droughts and heat waves will increase stress on water supplies and impact agriculture and food supply. Insect-borne diseases such as malaria will move northward as global temperatures rise, endangering more human lives.

IN HIGH DEMAND

Environmental engineering will grow faster between 2012 and 2022 than all other careers on average. In May 2012, an environmental engineer with a bachelor's degree earned an average annual salary of $80,890.[4] Engineering technicians with two-year associate's degrees will be needed to assist engineers and carry out day-to-day testing and maintain the systems environmental engineers design.

Environmental engineers will be needed to design environmentally sustainable structures and restore ecological sites harmed by human activities. Other experts will be needed to develop ways to efficiently recycle and dispose of electronic waste from discarded computers and other technologies. Environmental engineers will be asked to solve public health problems, such as designing freshwater delivery systems or decontaminating water supplies in developing countries. As cities grow, engineers will design more efficient means of transportation, sewage disposal, and other types of infrastructure.

Given the many emerging environmental issues resulting from human activities, future environmental engineers will likely lead efforts to preserve and protect the environment. They may help mitigate or prevent disasters such as the *Deepwater Horizon* oil spill or design solutions to meet the water crisis in Africa. Others may help nations prepare for the effects of climate change as engineers have in the Netherlands, preparing its extensive dike system for sea level rise as the climate warms.

CHAPTER 2

ENVIRONMENTAL ENGINEERING

Engineers in any discipline use the principles of science and mathematics to analyze, design, and develop solutions to technical problems. Some develop new products or designs. Others test and improve designs, oversee construction, and analyze problems. Because technical projects are varied and complex, engineers specialize in one or more areas, such as civil, electrical, or environmental engineering. Engineering fields often overlap with each other and with related sciences. A person might have a degree in civil, chemical, or mechanical engineering but work on environmental problems.

Environmental engineering is a challenging and rewarding field.

GENERAL DUTIES OF ENVIRONMENTAL ENGINEERS

An environmental engineer's duties vary considerably depending on the project at hand. Environmental engineers may:

- Prepare environmental investigation reports

- Design projects for environmental protection

- Update and maintain plans, permits, and operating procedures

- Provide technical support during environmental remediation

- Analyze scientific data and run quality-control checks

- Monitor progress of environmental projects

- Inspect facilities to ensure they are following environmental regulations

- Advise agencies on cleanup of contaminated sites

The title is less important than how the engineer's knowledge fits the specific problem.

WHAT ENVIRONMENTAL ENGINEERS DO

Environmental engineers use their knowledge of science and mathematics to develop solutions to environmental problems. Most have knowledge of biology, chemistry, or soil science. A background in other sciences is often essential, too. For example, an environmental engineer working on water issues may need knowledge of human health, oceanography, or hydrology, the study of water distribution and movement around the earth. Someone working on the cleanup of toxic waste sites would need to know geology and ecology as well as chemistry and soil science.

Some environmental engineers work on local issues, such as improving water quality or developing a metropolitan recycling center. Others tackle global issues such as climate change or atmospheric pollution. Because possible projects are so diverse, environmental engineers may work in a variety of settings, from offices to urban areas to wilderness sites.

HISTORY OF ENVIRONMENTAL ENGINEERING

As the global community continues to resolve environmental problems, environmental engineers will increasingly practice sustainable engineering to meet the goals of sustainable development. Sustainable development meets the needs of the present without compromising the ability of future generations to meet their own needs. Those who practice sustainable engineering will develop systems that balance the needs of the environment with economic and societal concerns. Sustainable engineering involves extending human use of natural resources into the indefinite future without running out of resources, decreasing quality of life, or destroying the environment.

PIONEERS IN GREEN CHEMISTRY

Joseph DeSimone, of the University of North Carolina, Chapel Hill, received the Presidential Green Chemistry Challenge Award. He developed a new family of nontoxic solvents, or substances that can dissolve other substances, that will reduce the use of hazardous chemicals in a variety of industries, from petroleum refining to pulp-and-paper manufacturing. Enrique Iglesia, professor of chemical engineering at the University of California, Berkeley, has 37 patents for new, environmentally friendly chemicals used in energy production and petrochemical synthesis.

This approach began with the UN Conference on the Human Environment, held in Stockholm, Sweden, in 1972. The conference added the environment to the UN's list of global problems and led to the creation of the UN Environment Programme. The same year, the Club of Rome, a group of 30 prominent people from ten countries, published an influential book called *The Limits to Growth*. Using mathematical modeling, the book warned that humans' unbridled use of natural resources could cause the collapse of civilization. They advocated for the consideration of Earth's carrying capacity, or the upper limit of human population the planet can support, in future decisions. The authors called this approach sustainable development.

Later UN actions solidified the concept of sustainable development and led to the development of sustainable environmental engineering principles. In 1987, the UN World

Commission on Environment and Development published a report called *Our Common Future*. It adopted the concept of sustainable development and led to the 1992 UN Conference on Environment and Development, also known as the Earth Summit, held in Rio de Janeiro, Brazil. The Earth Summit was the first attempt to integrate economic and environmental issues and set goals for the 2000s. At the 2002 World Summit on Sustainable Development in Johannesburg, South Africa, delegates adopted the Millennium Development Goals (MDGs) to reduce poverty and improve human life around the world. The most recent Earth Summit, in 2012 in Rio de Janeiro, Brazil, began developing a set of Sustainable Development Goals to provide guidelines for implementing sustainable development and meeting the MDGs.

The MDGs are interrelated, and almost every one requires the expertise of environmental engineers. For example, eradicating extreme poverty and hunger might involve developing a water delivery system to provide a poor region with clean water for drinking and agriculture. This will enable residents to grow more food. It would also decrease the incidence of disease, improving maternal health and lowering child mortality rates.

DIFFERENT TYPES OF ENVIRONMENTAL ENGINEERS

Environmental problems are complex and nearly always require engineers to work as part of a team, collaborating with experts who specialize in different areas. Typical environmental engineering projects include work with chemistry, geology, hydrology, and ecology. Some also involve elements of civil engineering.

Environmental engineers may find ways to deliver safe drinking water to communities in African countries.

Chemical environmental engineers analyze air, water, and soil pollution and use the data to develop methods to decrease amounts and toxicities of chemicals introduced into the environment by industries, power plants, and vehicles. They might remove chemicals from the waste stream or alter their toxicity before release. Some chemical engineers design new chemicals that are cleaner and less hazardous.

Engineers with geology training work on projects dealing with the intersection of air, water, soil, and organisms and the effects of human activities on all of these components. They might analyze and design solutions for pollution problems involving mining and groundwater contamination, waste management, or urban planning. They might deal with natural hazards, such as flooding, erosion, or impacts of hurricanes or earthquakes. Geological engineers use geologic data and principles in the planning and design of large-scale engineering projects such as dams, tunnels, bridges, mines, and buildings. They consult on environmental risks and safety for all projects.

Environmental engineers trained in hydrology solve water-related problems, from supplying water to keeping it clean to controlling its flow. They might analyze water samples for contaminants and figure out how to remove them or map watersheds and design systems for supplying water to people within them. They might build computer models to

EVERY JOB IS DIFFERENT

Environmental engineer Katie Goode loves math, science, and solving problems. She also enjoys the variety in her career. In one project, she traced pollution sources and advised industries on better engineering solutions. This was to help find a better way to manage storm-water runoff. She has worked in India, mapping impoverished areas for redevelopment. She's also worked in Uganda, helping design and construct a mill so a community could grind cassava, its staple crop.

predict flooding or determine how to prevent pollutants in underground storage tanks from leaking into groundwater. Many hydrological engineers deal with climate change impacts such as drought planning and optimizing water supplies.

As its name implies, ecological engineering combines the fields of ecology and engineering. It is a relatively new field closely related to sustainable engineering. Ecological engineering focuses on entire ecosystems, either restoring already damaged ecosystems or creating new, sustainable ones. Restoring or creating a new wetland is one example of an ecological engineering project. The restoration of a brownfield is another.

Civil engineers are concerned with what is called the built environment. The built environment includes buildings and other structures created by humans. Engineers may participate in the design and construction

Designing dike systems such as this one in the Netherlands requires the expertise of civil and environmental engineers.

of power plants or transportation systems. Or they may develop ways to sustainably use natural resources, design clean and efficient energy systems, or develop sustainable water supply systems. Any large structural system, from the Netherlands dikes to a local waste disposal plant, may require a civil or environmental engineer—who may be the same person.

The field of environmental engineering is highly diverse. A person with an interest in tackling any type of environmental problem is likely to find a niche in this field.

CHAPTER 3

THE *DEEPWATER* CLEANUP

Giant oil spills, including tanker spills and blowouts on oil rigs, account for only approximately 10 percent of oil entering the oceans.[1] However, these large, concentrated spills are the most devastating. They can kill marine organisms and damage ecosystems, sometimes for years to come. The *Deepwater Horizon* disaster will likely be no different. What's more, the rising world production and use of petroleum suggest the threat of oil spill disasters may increase in the future.

In July 2010, oil slicks could still be seen near the Transocean drilling rig where the *Deepwater Horizon* exploded.

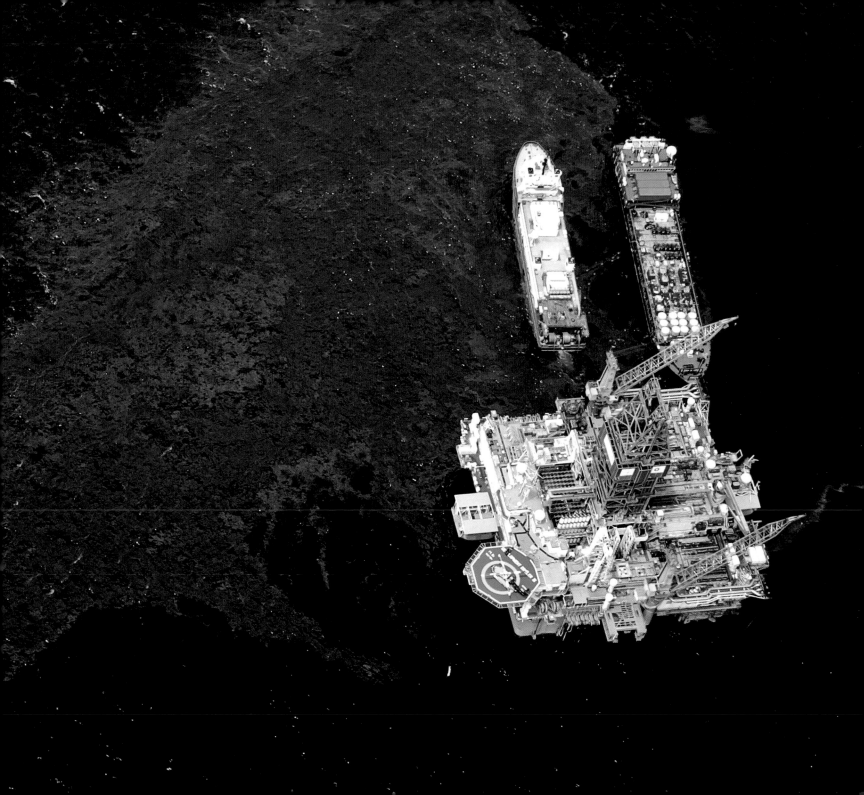

BP APPEARS UNPREPARED

Even the most efficient oil spill cleanups are messy and incomplete. But cleanup of the *Deepwater Horizon* spill is a cautionary tale, a story of what should have been done rather than what was done. It illuminates the deficiencies of current preparation and cleanup technologies, areas where future environmental engineers will likely study and improve.

According to investigations after the disaster, BP might have been able to prevent the disaster by managing its rig more responsibly before the spill. The investigations revealed BP management overlooked serious errors in well design, made inadequate repairs, and then failed to test them adequately. For example, investigators assert BP knowingly used a faulty BOP on the Macondo well, and, in the hours before the explosions, rig supervisors ignored warning signs, including seriously abnormal pressure readings. After the explosions, BP had difficulty stopping the oil from spilling into the Gulf of Mexico. It took 86 days to cap the well and stop the flow of oil. The first two methods the company tried, called "Top Hat" and "Top Kill," failed in testing in deep water during April and May, while the spill was already happening. In addition, BP inaccurately estimated the amount of oil flowing out. The cleanup technology BP used was surprisingly low-tech, especially compared to the technology used to extract the oil. Cutler J. Cleveland, writing for *The Encyclopedia of Earth*,

TIMELINE OF THE CLEANUP

- April 20: explosions and fire on the *Deepwater Horizon*
- April 22: sinking of the *Deepwater Horizon* rig
- April 25: BP fails to activate the BOP
- April 28: first controlled burn of oil slick
- May 7: BP's "Top Hat" efforts fail
- May 16: BP inserts tube and captures some oil and gas
- May 26: BP begins "Top Kill"
- May 29: "Top Kill" fails
- June 2: BP uses robots to cut off pipe and lower containment cap
- June 4: cap is containing 1,000 barrels per day[3]
- July 3: super tanker converted into "super skimmer" begins tests to remove surface oil
- July 12: BP installs more efficient "capping stack"
- July 15: BP announces leak has stopped

put the situation in perspective: "The three-month saga of BP's attempts to stem the flow of oil made it clear that the oil industry's impressive ability to extract oil from ever deeper offshore environments had not been accompanied by an equally effective capability to predict and respond to accidents."[2]

The oil spill occurred nearly 50 miles (80 km) off the coast of Louisiana. It eventually spread over nearly 29,000 square miles (75,000 sq km) of ocean, an area approximately the size of South Carolina.[4] Though the area affected changed daily with winds and currents, by early July, oil had reached the shores of all five Gulf States. Scientists also discovered huge clouds of oil in deep waters. By mid-August, approximately 57,540 square miles (149,028 sq km) of water were closed to fishing and 665 miles (1,070 km) of coastline were contaminated.[5] Before it was over, an estimated 207 million gallons (784 million L) of crude oil had poured into the Gulf of Mexico.[6] Some experts believed 210 million gallons (795 million L), or approximately 5 million barrels, had actually been spilled.[7]

BP was supposed to manage the cleanup, but it soon became clear the company was overwhelmed by the task. More than 20 federal agencies and five states stepped in to help. The cleanup eventually involved at least 6,400 vessels.[8] At the height of operations on July 8, approximately 47,000 people were employed in the cleanup operation.[9]

CLEANUP TECHNOLOGY

After an oil spill, many companies contract with the responsible party, BP in the case of the *Deepwater Horizon* spill, to develop a plan, provide equipment, and carry out a cleanup response. The people in charge of these services include environmental engineers, including scientists and

Crews burn off oil on the water's surface in the Gulf of Mexico in July 2010.

engineers with expertise in oil and gas technology, hazardous waste cleanup, and use of cleanup equipment.

The *Deepwater Horizon* cleanup used four types of technologies: booms, skimmers, controlled burns, and chemical dispersants. Booms are large, floating structures towed behind boats or placed in the water to contain oil. They corral surface oil to prevent it from entering sensitive areas or reaching beaches. Cleanup crews deployed more than 10.4 million feet (3.2 million m) of boom.[10] Engineers and crews used two types of booms to control the oil: a containment boom and sorbent boom. A containment boom has a float on top and a weighted bottom forming a "skirt" to contain the oil. Approximately 2.7 million feet (0.8 million m) of containment boom were used. A sorbent boom soaks up the oil. Its long, sausagelike strips of absorbent material are similar to disposable diaper filling. It lacks the underwater skirt and cannot hold oil for very long.[11] Cleanup crews used 8.7 million feet (2.7 million m) of sorbent boom to contain the spill.[12]

Skimmers, as the name implies, skim oil off the water surface and into containment structures. Often booms and skimmers are used together. The boom gathers and concentrates the oil into a confined area, and a skimmer removes it. During the cleanup, engineers from the company Water Planet Engineering, in cooperation with BP and other companies, retrofitted six oil spill response vehicles with specialized centrifuges that separated oil from the water. The centrifuges processed oily water collected by skimmers, reclaimed the crude oil for reprocessing, and discharged clean water back into the Gulf.

Cleanup engineers and crews also employed controlled burns and chemical dispersants in an effort to contain the spill. In the first few months of the spill, 411 controlled burns removed 11.4 million gallons (43.2 million L) of oil from the surface.[13] Controlled burns are used only in seas with waves of three feet (1 m) or less, where waters are calm enough to contain the oil. Chemical dispersants do not destroy or remove the oil. Instead, they break it into tiny particles, spreading it throughout the water from surface to floor. The goal is to prevent the oil from reaching the shore.

OIL IN THE OCEAN

During the first few hours and days after a spill, oil forms slicks on the water surface and undergoes physical and chemical processes that remove or disperse it. This process is called weathering. Oil forms surface slicks naturally, even without wind or wave action. Gravity and interaction between the oil and water molecules increase spreading, while the thickness of the oil, called viscosity, decreases it. Thus, light oil spreads more readily than heavier oil because light oil is thinner.

Weathering begins with evaporation. The lightweight, volatile oils evaporate most quickly, and approximately 80 percent of evaporation occurs within the first two days.[14] Other weathering processes include dissolving, sedimentation, biodegradation, and the formation of tar balls. Sedimentation is the accumulation of heavier oil on the ocean floor. Sedimented oil cannot be removed unless it is on or near shore, and then only with heavy equipment. In deep waters, the oil in sediments can only be removed by biodegradation—the slow breakdown of oil by

MILLIONS OF GALLONS

On August 10, 2010, the Unified Incident Command controlling the cleanup provided statistics on the spill. It assumed a total spill of 205.8 million gallons (779 million L), or 4.9 million barrels. In addition to the oil, the Unified Incident Command estimated as much as 95.6 million gallons (361.9 million L) of gasoline leaked.[15]

CHOCOLATE MOUSSE

A type of water-in-oil mixture occurs when strong waves or currents trap water inside oil droplets. It is called "chocolate mousse" because it resembles that dessert. These stable emulsions can quadruple the oil's volume. They may remain in the environment for months or years.

bacteria, fungi, and yeast. It is a natural, but not a short-term, solution for cleaning up spills. Heavy oil that has weathered at sea eventually forms tar balls or tar mats, flattened, pancakelike structures. Both accumulate along shorelines and must be removed by hand. Only a tiny percentage of lightweight oils dissolve. These dissolved compounds can be extremely toxic to aquatic life, but there is no way for an oil cleanup response to target them.

Every oil spill is different, and weathering processes differ. Environmental engineers and other responders must analyze each spill and determine the best approach to cleanup. The most effective responses occur when the oil slick is still on the water surface.

ENGINEERING CHALLENGES

Engineers must determine the size, direction, and speed of movement of an oil spill to handle it effectively. Spotters can track open-ocean oil spills visually from aircraft and helicopters, but this strategy is not as accurate as remote sensing from aircraft or satellites. Sensors include heat sensors and still and video cameras. Microwave and radar sensors can reveal relative thickness of a spill.

To calculate the amount of oil entering the water, engineers must have an accurate estimate of the flow rate, or rate at which the oil is leaking. Engineers did not have an accurate estimate of the *Deepwater Horizon* spill's flow rate. Early estimates of 1,000 to 5,000 barrels per day were based on visual observations of the oil slick and the two leaks from the pipe. Later, independent scientists used video footage of the leaks to calculate the spill's actual flow rate. The *Deepwater Horizon* disaster spilled 52,700 to 62,200 barrels of oil per day into the Gulf of Mexico.[16]

Advance planning, preparation, and responsible actions by oil rig owners and managers can prevent many oil spill problems. Engineers now use sophisticated computer models to predict the path of oil spills. They use information on types and amounts of oil, plus environmental data such as temperature and ocean currents, to calculate the rates of various weathering processes. Accurate models are important but limited by changing environmental conditions. With these tools, engineers should be able to prevent and mitigate oil spills.

FUTURE CLEANUPS

Three years after the *Deepwater Horizon* exploded, experts took stock of the situation. Was the cleanup successful? Had the Gulf of Mexico recovered? Answers vary. BP and the US government said yes, the cleanup was nearly complete and successful. But many people who live and work along the Gulf Coast disagreed. In the aftermath of the *Deepwater Horizon* spill, experts debated the benefits and costs of the cleanup methods used and oil spill cleanup technology that may be developed in the future.

Tar balls continued washing ashore in July 2010, three months after the *Deepwater Horizon* explosion.

THREE YEARS LATER: THE STATE OF THE GULF

As of June 2013, BP and the US Coast Guard officially ended their cleanup efforts in Mississippi, Alabama, and Florida. It continued monitoring approximately 84 miles (135 km) of Louisiana shoreline.[1] As of 2014, remaining work consisted of picking up tar balls from the beaches and drilling holes to find and remove tar mats buried under sand and sediment. In 2013, work crews with the US Coast Guard's Incident Management Team collected 4.6 million pounds (2.1 million kg) of oily material from the Gulf Coast shoreline. Since the spill in 2010, they have collected approximately 213 million pounds (96.6 million kg) of these substances.[2]

But, as cleaning efforts wind down, residents along the Gulf of Mexico still feel the effects of the spill. While some fish and shellfish harvests showed no major declines, the Louisiana fishing industry suffered severe losses. The state's oyster catch is down 27 percent. Some fishermen have gone out of business, and others are catching much less. George Barisich of Yscloskey, Louisiana, said his shrimp catch is 40 to 60 percent lower than it was before the spill.[3]

Dr. Samantha Joye of the University of Georgia leads a research group studying ecological effects of the spill. Joye points out that oil spills have both acute and chronic effects. Acute effects happened immediately and included the deaths of large marine animals—birds, sea turtles, and dolphins covered in oil. Joye and her team hope to obtain at least ten years of data showing chronic, or long-term, effects in order to describe the recovery process. For example, since the oil spill, instances of dolphins and sea turtles being stranded have increased, and there have been reports of deformed fish.

Rather than focusing on oil spill cleanup, government and industries are concentrating most of their efforts on spill prevention, including better industry oversight and new rules to improve the safety of deepwater drilling. They are not addressing the cleanup process. However, experts agree spills will happen despite our best efforts. Will we have the technology and engineering expertise to respond adequately to them?

OIL CLEANUP ON SHORELINES

The most common shoreline cleanup method is manual recovery, in which teams of workers remove oil with gloved hands, shovels, buckets, and sorbent materials. They collect the oil in plastic bags or barrels for removal. Specialized beach-cleaning equipment and front-end loaders are used for larger spills. Small vacuum systems remove oil from pools. Shorelines are sometimes washed with low-pressure warm or cool water. Chemical beach cleaners, containing surfactants and low-toxicity solvents, may be added to the water.

CURRENT TECHNOLOGIES: BOOMS AND SKIMMERS

Dr. Robert Bea, a former oil tanker captain and currently professor emeritus of civil and environmental engineering at the University of California, Berkeley, says booms work well in calm waters, but their effectiveness in open, choppy waters is slight at best. Even under normal conditions, oil migrates under booms because it is often heavier than water after mixing with sediment, debris, or cleanup chemicals. Poorly designed booms can tip from vertical to nearly horizontal, allowing oil to pass over or under them, and strong wind, waves, or floating debris can cause structural failure.

Most skimmers are designed to handle either light, medium, or heavy oil. No single skimmer can handle all situations. Poor weather, clogging by debris, oil viscosity, the spreading rate of oil slicks, and waves and currents all limit the recovery of oil with skimmers. Best results occur when oil is concentrated; thus, early arrival at the spill site is the best guarantee of success.

CURRENT TECHNOLOGIES: CONTROLLED BURNS AND CHEMICAL DISPERSANTS

During controlled burns, the oil is surrounded with a fireproof boom and set on fire. This solution is efficient and completely removes large

Dr. Robert Bea is known as the United States' foremost forensic engineer and was described by one magazine as the "Master of Disaster." He has analyzed more than 600 major engineering failures. Bea is a professor emeritus of the Department of Civil and Environmental Engineering at the University of California, Berkeley, and cofounder of the nonprofit Center for Catastrophic Risk Management. Bea is also codirector of the Marine Technology and Management Group Center for Risk Mitigation at the University of California, Berkeley.

Bea has worked as an engineer in the public and private sectors. He has designed oil platforms and pipelines and participated in construction, operations, maintenance, assessment, and management of oil engineering systems worldwide. Two of Bea's high-profile projects are the investigations of levee failures after Hurricane Katrina and the *Deepwater Horizon* oil spill.

Bea has designed oil platforms similar to this or

HELP FROM HOLLYWOOD

Some of the most technologically advanced methods in the *Deepwater Horizon* cleanup came not from the oil industry, but from two high-profile entertainers. James Cameron, Oscar-winning director of movies including *Titanic* and *The Abyss*, offered BP the use of his private fleet of remotely operated vehicles that operate at great depths. Since the 1990s, actor Kevin Costner has funded a team of scientists to create an oil-water separating device. Costner provided BP with 32 of the machines, which separate oil from water at a rate of 200 gallons (757 L) per minute, leaving the water more than 99 percent oil-free.[4] However, the US Coast Guard later said Costner's machines were not able to separate weathered oil from water during the spill.

amounts of oil. But controlled burns have disadvantages. The slick must be thick enough to burn, and burns must be done before the oil spreads to be effective. When a slick burns, it produces black smoke that contains soot and hydrocarbon byproducts, polluting the atmosphere.

The use of chemical dispersants in oil-spill cleanup is highly controversial. Dispersants contain chemicals like those in soaps and detergents, called surfactants, which break oil into tiny particles and mix it with the water below. The intent is to increase the natural rate of oil dispersion and prevent oil slicks from reaching coastlines. Their effectiveness varies, depending on the type of oil, degree of weathering, salt content of the water, water temperature, and type and amount of dispersant applied. When waves are low, more dispersant is required.

BP sprayed dispersants on surface slicks and also released them directly into the oil gushing from the pipe. Ultimately, they injected nearly 800,000 gallons (3 million L) of dispersant deep into the ocean.[5] The oil was definitely dispersed, but, while industry engineers see this as a solution, others see it as a problem. It spreads oil throughout the water column, instead of keeping it near the surface. This means less risk to large, visible animals such as seabirds and dolphins, but much greater risk to underwater organisms such as fish, plankton, coral reefs, clams, and oysters. A study published in February 2013 showed a mixture of oil and the dispersant used in the cleanup is 52 times more toxic to certain plankton than oil or dispersant alone.[6] This has serious implications because plankton form the base of food webs in the Gulf of Mexico.

THE FUTURE OF OIL CLEANUP TECHNOLOGY

The *Deepwater Horizon* spill jump-started cleanup research. Booms and skimmers still carry out most cleanup efforts, usually aided by dispersants or burning. Alternative methods include chemical dispersants and controlled burning. The most important new technique, according to Ken Lee of Canada's Centre for Offshore Oil, Gas, and Energy Research, may

Peat moss grows in bogs. An 11-pound (5 kg) bag of it can soak up 8 gallons (30 L) of oil.

be bioremediation techniques. These techniques let nature do the cleanup work by allowing bacteria and fungi to break down the oil. Bioremediation may be the easiest, cheapest, and most effective approach. Another nature-based technology is peat moss. When placed directly in oily water, it soaks up oil but not water. A Norwegian company is developing the peat product.

Engineers and scientists are making progress in oil spill cleanup technology, but there is a long way to go. In the near future, it appears standard methods will prevail. While new, innovative methods are still being developed, creative solutions to problems such as oil cleanup in underwater environments are greatly needed. Oil spills are not the only water projects environmental engineers tackle, however. Engineers also address freshwater pollution and develop new technologies that give people across the globe access to clean water.

NEW TECH

In 2011, Elastec/American Marine won $1.4 million in a competition sponsored by the X Prize Foundation for new oil spill technology with its grooved disc skimmer. The new skimmer skims 4,670 gallons (17,680 L) of oil per minute, compared to the industry standard of 1,100 gallons (4,200 L) per minute.[7]

CHAPTER 5

OVERCOMING WATER SCARCITY

Fatoumata grew up in Mali, in sub-Saharan West Africa, in a village without water or sanitation. The oldest of seven children, she was responsible for caring for her siblings and supplying the family's water. Every day, she got up at 4:00 a.m., hiked to the nearest water source, filled containers with water, and hiked back. The journey was a long one. Fatoumata recalled that "when I got back, my baby siblings would be crying because they were so thirsty."[1] During the dry season, she and fellow villagers often traveled many miles to find water. But with the help of a teacher, Fatoumata stayed in school and received

Some women in Africa walk long distances to find water.

a scholarship to study abroad. Today, she works for the organization WaterAid, bringing water and sanitation to villages in Mali.

Every day, women and girls throughout sub-Saharan Africa walk to the nearest water source, usually a river or hand-dug well. There, they fill water jugs and plastic buckets with brown water. They carefully place the filled containers weighing more than 40 pounds (18 kg) on their heads and begin the long, tiring trek home. Girls often miss school to help carry water. They walk ten miles (16 km) or more per day, often in darkness or through dangerous areas where they may be violently attacked.[2] The water they carry supplies one day's drinking, cooking, and washing needs. It is often muddy and contaminated with human waste, but it is all they have. Across Africa, women and children spend 40 billion hours per year collecting water this way.[3]

One of today's greatest environmental challenges is supplying clean, reliable water resources to people in developing countries, particularly in Africa. Environmental engineers will need to find solutions to reduce water scarcity and address other water problems common in Africa.

HOW SERIOUS IS THE WATER PROBLEM?

The National Academy of Engineering lists access to clean water as one of the "grand challenges for engineering."[4] As of 2012, lack of clean water

WORLD WATER SCARCITY

The UN designated the decade from 2005 to 2015 as the UN International Decade for Action: Water for Life. One of the UN's MDGs is to reduce the number of people without safe drinking water and sanitation by half. Although the world has reached the MDG target for improved water access, at least 768 million people still lack access to safe drinking water, and 1 billion lack toilets.[7] The UN keeps statistics on global water scarcity.

- In the twentieth century, water use grew twice as fast as population.[8]

- Water scarcity currently affects 20 percent of the world's people.[9]

- By 2025, 1.8 billion people will live in countries with water scarcity.[10]

- In 2013, almost 2.5 billion people, including 1 billion children, lacked basic sanitation, causing a child to die every 20 seconds.[11]

has caused more deaths worldwide than war. One of every six people lacks access to clean water and one in three lacks basic sanitation. Nearly 5,000 children die every day from diarrhea-related illnesses, due primarily to lack of sanitation.[5] According to a report by the UN Development Programme, "Overcoming the crisis in water and sanitation is one of the greatest human development challenges of the early 21st century."[6] Environmental engineers are needed to help solve the global water crisis.

Although plenty of water is available on Earth, it is not always located where it is most needed. The Middle East and northern Africa, for example, often lack sufficient water, and the available water is usually contaminated. A water scarcity situation exists when a region has too little water to supply normal human requirements, or 1,310 cubic yards (1,000 cu m) of water per person. A region is water stressed when supplies fall below 2,220 cubic yards (1,700 cu m) per person per year. Currently, almost 2 billion of the world's 7 billion people suffer from extreme water scarcity.[12] This number will increase as population and resource consumption grow and climate change intensifies.

IMPLICATIONS OF WATER SCARCITY

The most obvious problem associated with water scarcity or contamination is human disease. Diseases spread by contaminated drinking water include cholera, typhoid, dysentery, and hepatitis. Typhus, skin infections, and trachoma, an eye disease causing blindness, occur when hygiene is poor due to water scarcity. Insects that live or breed in water spread other diseases, including malaria and dengue fever. Poor water, sanitation, and hygiene are responsible for 88 percent of diarrhea cases.[13] Because diarrhea causes dehydration, it can be fatal. It is the second-largest killer of children in the world today.[14]

Water scarcity also has a profound effect on agriculture. It takes approximately 70 percent of a region's water to grow crops. Producing a single apple requires 18.5 gallons (70 L) of water. A cow requires 52.8 gallons (200 L) to create one glass of milk, and 634 gallons (2,400 L) are needed to produce one hamburger from beef cattle.[15] Lack of water results in less food to feed growing populations. With a safe, clean water supply, people can increase crop production and improve nutrition, thereby improving their health.

In general, water scarcity prevents people from improving their quality of life and achieving basic goals, such as education or economic

Contaminated water can cause typhoid and cholera.

improvement. Its greatest impact is on women and girls. Across Africa, women are responsible for household and child-care tasks. This includes water collection, which often takes up to eight hours per day. Women must carry water by hand or on their heads, which leads to physical problems. However, these tasks are not considered "work" by governments. Thus, women's needs are not typically considered when governments make decisions on issues such as transportation or water supply.

AFRICA'S WATER PROBLEM: ENGINEERING CHALLENGES

Africa's water problems are as vast as the continent. One engineering challenge is the lack of infrastructure, particularly in rural regions. The World Bank cites poor infrastructure as a significant barrier limiting Africa's growth. Harvard University professor Calestous Juma specifies a need to invest heavily in rural roads, electrification, and

MOVING WATER

Some simple inventions have eased the burden of women and children who walk long distances each day carrying heavy loads of water. Social entrepreneur Cynthia Koenig designed the Wello WaterWheel, a water barrel with handles that holds up to 25 gallons (97 L) of water. It can be pushed or pulled, even over rough ground.[16] A similar invention now used in rural South Africa is the Imvubu, or "hippo." The Imvubu is a rolling water barrel that holds 24 gallons (90.8 L).[17]

irrigation. He points out the percentage of rural Africans living within 1.24 miles (2 km) of an all-weather road ranges from approximately 32 percent in Kenya to only 10.5 percent in Ethiopia.[18] Lack of roads isolates rural people. It also limits the transportation of heavy equipment for large-scale engineering projects into these areas. Without electricity, electric water pumps are useless. Though lack of infrastructure limits some solutions, it can encourage small, decentralized, ecologically sound solutions for water distribution and purification.

To develop a successful water delivery or treatment system in a water-scarce African nation, environmental engineers must plan to ensure the project's viability after construction is completed. Often, well-intentioned individuals or members of nongovernmental organizations (NGOs) begin water projects. They raise money, dig wells or build other facilities, and leave. When the structure breaks or runs dry and villagers cannot repair it, communities return to drinking contaminated water from the local river.

GEOGRAPHIC AND CLIMATIC CHALLENGES

The Azawak region is a vast, dry plain the size of Florida. It is located in the Sahel region of West Africa, on the southern edge of the Sahara Desert. With a dry season lasting approximately ten months, its harsh

INVOLVING THE COMMUNITY

In Ethiopia, Laura Brunson develops water filtration methods to remove toxins including arsenic and fluoride. Her filters use locally available materials, such as bone or wood char. Through community surveys, she discovered that some communities have religious objections to filtering water through bone char. Consulting villagers and determining their needs and wishes enabled her to prevent wasted work and develop a product that villagers would use.

climate causes permanent water scarcity for the region's 500,000 people.[19] Coupled with insufficient food and inadequate infrastructure and health care, the Azawak people consistently face life-threatening conditions. Half of all children under five die of thirst or water-scarcity diseases every year.

At the southern end of the continent is the Republic of South Africa. Its northernmost area is Limpopo Province, one of the country's poorest regions. In 2013, 74.2 percent of Limpopo's people lived in poverty and 48.5 percent were destitute.[20] Though Limpopo's landscape is varied, only 32 percent of children there have drinking water on site, and only 24 percent have access to basic sanitation.[21] Limpopo's greatest need is for sustainable systems that will provide a steady supply of clean, potable water.

Major challenges for supplying water for Africa require tackling water scarcity, water contamination, and sanitation. Problems must be solved against the backdrop of minimal infrastructure, local cultures, and harsh physical environments. Despite these challenges, environmental engineers and other experts are developing ways to handle Africa's water crisis.

Girls bring home water in the Limpopo Province of South Africa in 2012.

ENGINEERING SUCCESSES

Environmental engineers measure a project's success by whether the system continues functioning after it is put in place. But, according to the World Health Organization, up to 60 percent of water projects in the developing world do not function as they are intended to. This strongly suggests a need for a new approach. Currently, an approach involving small-scale village initiatives is being tried. Several projects are designed to respond to specific needs of people in small areas. They use simple technology based on locally available supplies and are geared toward local control of the system.

Many projects in Africa bring water to rural communities.

SUPPLYING WATER IN THE DESERT

It can take the help of organizers and activists to put the ideas of environmental engineers into action. Amman Imman (Water is Life) is the brainchild of Ariane Kirtley, who became aware of the plight of Niger's Azawak region while conducting public health research. She witnessed children traveling 30 miles (50 km) per day to search for water. Kirtley met families who had hand-dug wells 300 feet (90 m) deep without reaching water.[1] She spoke with cattle herders whose animals had died over the past decade because the rainy season had dwindled from five months to one month per year. The Azawak region was receiving no assistance from governments or NGOs. In 2006, Kirtley formed Amman Imman, a nonprofit humanitarian organization, with the help of family and friends.

Kirtley's goal is to tap the huge aquifer underlying the Azawak region. Clean, abundant water is available 600 to 3,000 feet (180 to 910 m) below the surface, under sand and bedrock.[2] She plans to provide a series of oases across the Azawak by drilling boreholes into the aquifer in key locations. Between 2006 and 2012, Amman Imman completed boreholes in four villages. When the wells were completed, residents began pursuing previously impossible activities, including farming, reforestation, education, and economic development.

Drilling a borehole requires a drilling rig mounted on a truck. Rotary drill bits used near the surface remove soft soil, and deeper down, percussion bits break through bedrock. Water is pumped through the borehole pipe into a metal storage tank and delivered through faucets to individuals. Horizontal pipes feed water to tanks supplying the livestock. Villagers help set up the water tank and lay the pipe. Since its completion in 2007, the Tangarwashane borehole has supplied water during the dry season to approximately 25,000 people and animals.[3] The communities served by the borehole include four villages and several nomad camps. Other boreholes have had similar success, and the project continues.

MOVING WATER SHORT DISTANCES

Some regions of Africa have sufficient rainfall for at least part of the year, but lack plentiful, clean water year-round. Countries have no systems to catch, store, and disperse the water in villages or

SUCCESSFUL WATER PROJECTS

A successful water project in a developing country requires careful planning and preparation. Community members should participate from the beginning. Environmental engineers first complete a site investigation, testing the water source and determining the best place for a water system. Then they develop a preliminary design, plan a budget, and secure funding in advance. If possible, engineers use local materials to support the local community. During construction, community members receive training in building techniques, such as concrete work, pipe fitting, and erosion control. They also learn to maintain the system after it becomes operational.

rural areas, so communities must collect it from open, often contaminated, sources and carry it long distances home.

One engineering solution to this problem is to build simple gravity-fed systems, in which water runs downhill into a permanent storage tank. This eliminates the need for pumps in areas lacking electricity and enables residents to store water, saving time and providing a more reliable water supply. Gravity-fed systems are inexpensive to build with simple, locally available materials and manual labor. Covered spring systems are used in the Lowveld region of South Africa, which includes the Limpopo Valley. In rural areas, springs are often the most reliable water source. If a community is already using a spring, its water can be made cleaner and more accessible, and if a gravity-flow system is built around the spring, water can be stored. Such a system also decreases water-borne diseases such as cholera and dysentery and mosquito-borne diseases such as malaria.

Different organizations are bringing gravity-fed water systems to the Lowveld region. Engineer Richard Wareham founded the nonprofit SunStove Organization to make his simple solar cooker available and help people in undeveloped countries feed their families. As part of this organization's outreach in the Lowveld, SunStove has also helped build 1,400 low-tech gravity-fed water systems to bring clean water to more than 41,000 families.[4] Civil and environmental engineers design the systems. College students and volunteers help build them. However, the goal is for local citizens to be involved in designing, building, and maintaining them. Otherwise, the systems may be abandoned once they fail or the builders leave.

BUILDING A GRAVITY-FED SYSTEM

While gravity-fed systems are good potential sources of drinking water, developing a spring requires a careful building process. Springs are subject to surface contamination because they are fed by shallow groundwater. Water in a gravity-fed system should always be tested. In most cases, it will need to be treated before drinking. The best springs to develop are concentrated springs, which have a single, visible outflow point. This point is called the spring eye. They often occur along hillsides where groundwater seeps through cracks in the bedrock. Concentrated springs are usually less contaminated and have higher flow rates.

RAIN CATCHMENT SYSTEMS

Another gravity-flow system, the rain catchment system, is a good supplementary water source, extending water availability into the dry season. In this system, rainwater travels down an angled roof into gutters and is captured in a permanent storage container on the ground. Either the roof or storage container may contaminate the water. To prevent roof contamination, builders install filters on the gutters or devices to divert the refuse that runs off the roof in the first burst of rainfall. Then the systems can collect clean rainwater. Storage containers should not have previously stored fuels, pesticides, or other toxins.

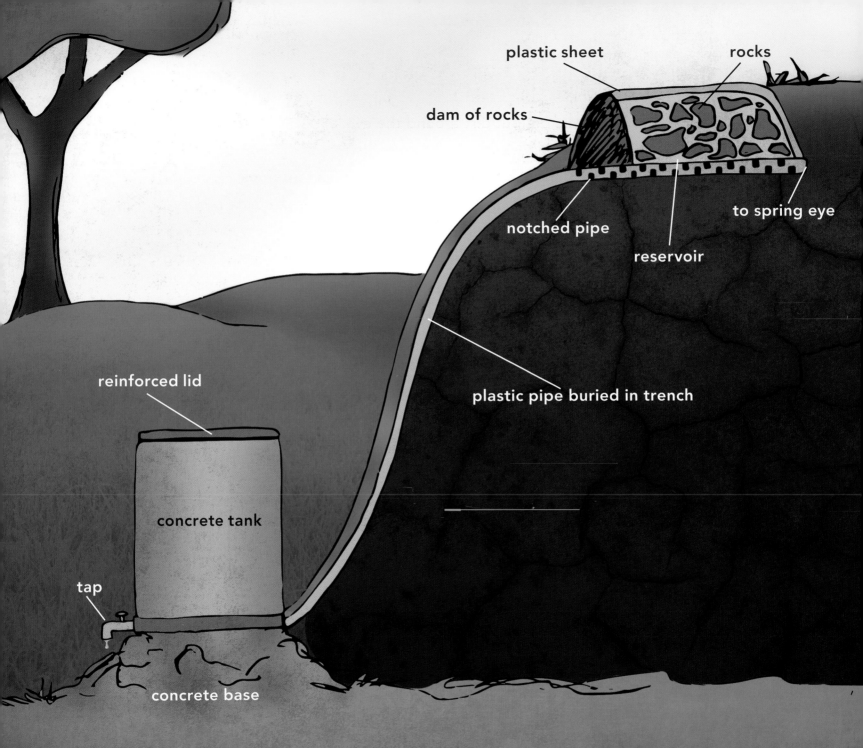

First, engineers dig out dirt around the eye, allowing flowing water to clean it. Then, they bury a notched pipe near the spring eye. Over it, they build a small dam of rocks, creating a reservoir. The reservoir is covered with a plastic sheet. Next, they dig a trench with a plastic pipe laid in, connected to the notched pipe, leading to a storage tank. Water flows into a concrete tank with a tap installed at its base. For a faster-flowing stream, a box with a sloped top to encourage runoff is placed over the spring eye.

PURIFYING WATER: BIOSAND FILTRATION

Many people in Venda, a rural part of the Limpopo region, lack access to clean drinking water. Some villagers install pipes carrying water from a mountain river into their homes. The water is contaminated with bacteria and parasites. Engineering students from the University of Virginia collaborated with students from the University of Venda to build a slow sand filtration system to improve the quality of the river water. The system filtered water from existing pipes and stored it in a central location, where it was accessible to all community members. Ten community members volunteered to construct and maintain the system.

A slow sand filtration unit consists of layers of gravel and sand, topped by a thin biological layer through which the water travels. As it moves, bacterial action and adsorption by sand grains remove most contaminants. To be effective, water must flow constantly and slowly through the filter, providing oxygen and food to the bacteria.

Similar to slow sand filtration, biosand filtration units for individual households are also effective and simple to make. In these units, dirty water is simply poured into the top and run through biosand inside the unit. Clean water exits at the bottom. Studies show that a slow biosand filtration unit removes more than 90 percent of bacteria and 100 percent of parasites.[5] Various organizations are sponsoring the installation of slow biosand filters in Africa. As of 2011, 10,517 household units were installed in Zambia.[6] An additional 4,230 were placed in Kenya.[7]

SOLAR PERSONAL WATER PURIFICATION

Some innovative designs use solar energy to purify water. The Life Sack, developed by industrial designers Jung Uk Park, Myeong Hoon Lee, and Dae Youl Lee, looks like a large, clear, plastic bag. Life Sack uses the sun to naturally purify water. Once poured into Life Sack, water is placed in direct sunlight for at least six hours. The sun's heat and ultraviolet light kill the bacteria that cause diarrhea.

A recent development from the Indian Institute of Technology Madras uses nanoparticles to filter water. The nanoparticle filters remove both

SPOUTS OF WATER

Harvard University student Kathy Ku combined her engineering skills with her idealism to spearhead construction of a self-sustaining water filter factory in Uganda. Ten million people in Uganda lack clean water, approximately one-third of the country's population.[8] More than a dozen students carried out the project, called "Sustainable Point-of-Use Treatment and Storage (SPOUTS) of Water." The SPOUTS of Water factory manufactures clay filters. People in Uganda already cool water in terra-cotta pots. Using clay to store and clean water is familiar to them. The factory will employ 14 local workers and supply filters to Ugandan households for half the cost of imported filters.

microbes and chemical contaminants such as lead and arsenic. Because the filters are separate, the device can remove microbes, chemicals, or both. Though innovative, designing filters and other purification systems is only the beginning. Environmental engineers must also find ways to successfully implement and maintain these systems in the face of local and regional challenges such as lack of infrastructure, low education levels, political instability, and violence.

HOLDING BACK THE SEA

The Netherlands is a small European country located on the coast of the North Sea. It is approximately the size of Massachusetts and Connecticut combined, with a population of 16.8 million in 2013.[1] Most of the country is a delta formed by the mouths of the Rhine, Meuse, and Scheldt Rivers. More than one-fourth of its land area, home to more than 60 percent of its people, lies below sea level.[2] The Dutch have spent more than 2,000 years trying to protect the Netherlands from floods.

The Dutch have held back the sea by building dikes and in the process have become expert engineers. A dike, often called a levee in

The Dutch have tried for centuries to hold back the North Sea with dikes such as this one.

the United States, is a human-made embankment designed to keep a river or ocean from overflowing and flooding the land. Building dikes or levees is a job for both civil and environmental engineers. Engineers must have a thorough knowledge of the body of water and its movement. They must understand the geology, ecology, and soils of the area. They must be able to predict the dike's impact on the surrounding environment and apply sustainable building practices to minimize these impacts.

A dike can be made of anything as long as it holds back the water. Some dikes are made of piles of sand or soil, plant materials, rocks, or cement. They usually run in miles-long strips along the body of water they are meant to contain. In some areas of the Netherlands, the Dutch have also formed polders. Polders are new land areas reclaimed from the sea. They are made by building large, circular dikes and then pumping out all the salt water within the dike's walls.

Netherlands settlers built the first dikes approximately 2,000 years ago, using blocks of sod piled upon one another. At first, they built homes and villages on artificial hills called terps. Later, they connected the terps with long walls to protect their farmland. These walls were the first dikes. Early dikes were low, slanted mounds made of clay. Throughout the Middle Ages, many were made of pressed eelgrass, a type of marine plant. The first eelgrass dikes probably protected just a few farms. Later, larger

STRUCTURE OF A MODERN DIKE

A typical modern dike consists of a dike body and a covering to decrease the rate of erosion. The dike body will settle over time, so materials must be somewhat flexible. The underwater bank prevents erosion of the underside of the dike. It is covered with synthetic cloth and a layer of stones. The underwater platform supporting the dike body is usually sand or gravel. A row of poles sunk at the foot of the dike prevents upper layers from shifting down. A layer of basalt or cement blocks over coarse sand forms a filter that absorbs waves and allows water to quickly reenter the sea. Above the filter is a water-resistant asphalt layer. The asphalt is covered with clay and planted with grass to hold the clay in place.

structures protected several villages, and eventually dikes surrounded entire regions. Larger structures were probably reinforced with clay and sand. While the dikes provided more land for farmers, they also cut off access to the sea. The Dutch began building canals and waterways through the dikes to make shipping easier. Beginning in the 1600s, they began reinforcing dikes with rows of poles along their seaward sides and building breakwaters perpendicular to each dike to support it.

Improvements in the Netherlands dike system were usually made after catastrophes. In 1739, the great shipworm, a wood-boring clam, caused major damage to the Netherlands' dikes. The Dutch began building smaller sleeping dikes behind major ones to absorb some of the sea's energy. The inner row of sleeping dikes could stop the remaining waves that made it through the main dike system, thus preventing major disasters. The tidal flood of 1825 led to a redesign of the dike system. New dikes had sloped inclines and were strengthened with stones and sections of heavy basalt rock. In 1916, when a huge storm destroyed a major area along the Zuider Zee coasts, the Dutch built their dikes

The Dutch village of Oude Tonge was flooded after a large storm in February 1953.

higher and stronger. They rebuilt the system to "Zuiderzee height," approximately 14 feet (4.3 m) above Amsterdam, and closed off a large portion of this coast from the Wadden Sea.[3] The most recent catastrophe occurred in 1953, when a heavy storm breached 89 dikes and floods killed 1,835 people.[4] This storm provided the catalyst for a building project that lasted through the last half of the 1900s and resulted in today's dike system.

TODAY'S DIKE SYSTEMS

The Netherlands completed the Zuiderzee Works and Delta Works dike systems in the 2000s. Zuider Zee was originally a shallow bay of the North Sea, only 15 feet (4.6 m) deep but covering nearly 2,000 square miles (5,200 sq km). The Zuiderzee Works, begun in 1918, completely enclosed the Zuider Zee from the sea with a 20-mile- (32 km) long dam across the bay. The base of the dam was made of layers of sand and glacial till, a mixture of clay and small boulders. It was coated with basalt rock and willow branches, and covered with a final layer of sand and till. The dam's surface was planted with grass to slow erosion. Finally, a road was built along its top, and 25 gates to control water flow, called sluices, were added. The dikes were completed in 1933, and Zuider Zee became a freshwater lake, IJsselmeer. Before the dikes were completed, the Dutch started creating polders. From 1929 to 1967, 895 square miles

DESIGNING A NEW SYSTEM

After the flood of 1953, the Dutch completely redesigned their flood-control system. Their new approach includes:

- long-term thinking (designing for a 1-in-10,000-year storm)

- relying less on huge, solid dikes and more on natural ways to absorb floodwater

- using new synthetic textiles to prevent soil movement and water penetration

- using better monitoring systems, including automated systems with fiber-optic and electronic sensors

(2,318 sq km) of the lake were turned into polders for new farmland.[5]

The second system, built after the 1953 flood, is the Delta Works. The American Society of Civil Engineers considers it one of the seven wonders of the modern world. It consists of 13 dams and related structures, including barriers, sluices, locks, and 10,250 miles (16,496 km) of dikes. The dams form freshwater lakes and regulate water flow between the Rhine, Meuse, and Scheldt Rivers and the North Sea. Completed in 1997, the project shortened the coastline and resulted in 435 fewer miles (700 km) of dikes.[6] In addition to flood control, the Delta Works provides freshwater for drinking and irrigation, improves traffic between islands, and adds employment and recreational activities.

The largest Delta Works dam, the Eastern Scheldt storm surge barrier, is the largest storm surge barrier in the world. This open dam has

62 sluice gates, each a steel door that is 138 feet (42 m) wide.[7] The gates are normally left open and water moves freely through them, preserving the natural environment. They close during storms to provide flood control. To build the barrier, engineers first created an artificial island in the middle of the estuary where the barrier sits. Ships assisted in the Eastern Scheldt's construction. Its expected life-span is 200 years.

The Netherlands' latest effort to hold back the North Sea: the enormous Eastern Scheldt storm surge barrier.

THE DEADLY MUSKRAT

Many unusual factors can cause damage to a dam. Sometimes muskrats burrow into dikes to create nesting chambers, weakening the structure and increasing the likelihood of a breach. Willem van Dijk oversees dikes in the Dutch province of Flevoland. Every morning, he deploys 11 muskrat hunters armed with metal cages and spring traps baited with carrots. Van Dijk receives regular complaints that killing the muskrats is cruel and unnecessary. But muskrat hunter Jacko Westerndorp says, "We have to do this work. If the water comes, we all drown."[8]

ENGINEERING A DIKE

A dike must be stable so it does not collapse under strong water pressure, but it also must allow water to drain quickly. Thus, dikes usually have a water-impermeable layer, such as clay, on both sides, but permeable cores for drainage. This makes them both strong and flexible. Beyond these essentials, dike design varies depending on local factors, such as type of ground, materials available, strength needed, and local customs and traditions. Dutch engineers use probability to develop a final design. They evaluate the relative importance of all factors, including design, structure, economics, and safety. They take measurements and try to predict the likelihood of the failure of different designs. Then they choose an optimal design based on all these factors.

Dike design depends on three major factors: technical safety, functional analysis, and methods for maintenance. Engineers design dikes to avoid technical disasters, such as the failure of a dike during a storm. Engineers perform a functional analysis to study the factors required for the dike to perform properly. For example, the dike's crest height must be higher than the water level for which it is designed. The outer layer should be impermeable to limit leakage, while the inner layer should be permeable to permit drainage during an overflow. Buildings are allowed on dikes as long as they do not affect how the dike controls floods. Dike maintenance involves monitoring the dike regularly to compare its actual condition with its expected or required condition. If there is a difference, maintenance workers must take quick action to repair the problem.

DIKE SAFETY PHILOSOPHY

Dutch engineers assume some failures are inevitable in a highly technological society. Therefore, they base dike safety standards on the probability of failure during different events, such as powerful storms. The standards are based on the likelihood of the highest water levels occurring in a given year. For rivers, there is one chance in 1,250 that the highest water level will occur in a given year. Put another way, such high water levels are likely to occur only once in 1,250 years.[9]

CHAPTER 8

GEARING UP FOR CLIMATE CHANGE

Despite centuries of dike development, climate change puts the Netherlands at risk from sea level rise, increased river flow, and stronger storms. These effects will intensify in the coming decades. More than half of the Netherlands is already flood prone, and a 2006 study revealed that at least one-fourth of current dikes and other defenses need improvements.[1] The Netherlands will need to adapt its strategies for flood control in the future. Engineers in the United States may investigate how these strategies may be used in low-lying US cities such as New Orleans, Louisiana.

Low-lying New Orleans, Louisiana, *top left*, may benefit from engineering solutions developed in the Netherlands.

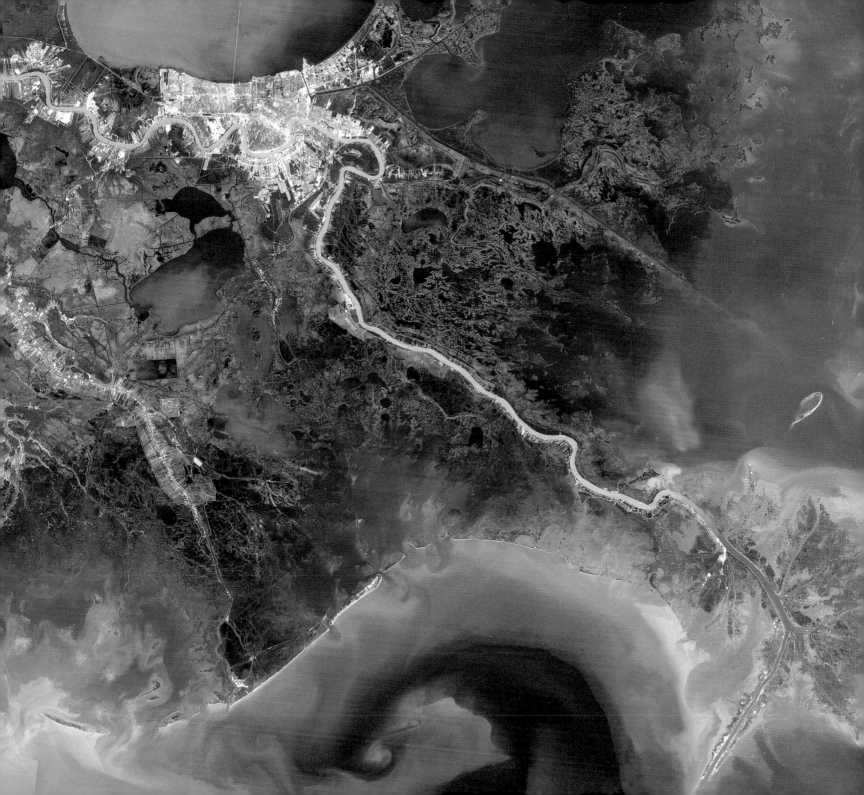

A NEW DIRECTION

The realities of climate change are causing the Netherlands to rethink its flood-control plan. It will continue repairing its dike systems and other hard defenses, such as the recently completed Delta Works, and it will add to them as the sea level rises. But hard defenses are very expensive and take decades to complete. As climate change accelerates, the Netherlands is considering alternative solutions to flood control. Engineers are embracing softer solutions that work with nature, rather than against it. As Ted Sluijter, spokesman for the Eastern Scheldt storm surge barrier, says, "If you fight nature, nature is going to strike back. Water needs space."[2]

The Netherlands' new soft approach, agreed to after much debate, involves ecological engineering. One proposed technique is to restore wetlands, beaches, and natural floodplains, all of which absorb water and energy from waves and storm surges. Opening some dikes would allow flooding on underproductive farmland, restoring it to wetlands. Newly flooded land would absorb carbon, and farmers would receive money for their contribution to decreasing greenhouse gases (and thus climate change). These methods are cheaper and, in the long run, likely more effective than hard defenses. They are also more ecologically sound.

SAND ENGINES AND SMART DIKES

The *zandmotor*, "sand engine," is a gigantic example of ecological engineering. Completed in 2011, this pile of sand 28 million cubic yards (21 million cubic m) in volume reaches half a mile (0.8 km) into the sea and protects a 12-mile (19 km) stretch of coastline in south-central Holland.[3] A massive operation dredged sand from offshore, where it had eroded from the coastline. Dredging crews deposited the sand back on shore, forming a crescent-shaped peninsula. Over the coming years, wind, waves, and tides will redistribute the sand along the beach, acting as a sand engine that will continually move the sand 15 miles (24 km) along the coast. Previously, this shoreline was replenished by dredging every five years, at great expense to both the economy and offshore ecosystems. Though the initial effort was immense in scale, the *zandmotor* will protect the shoreline

LIVING WITH WATER

In a Dutch harbor off the Meuse River, in the city of Rotterdam, sits the Floating Pavilion. Its three transparent domes, each three stories high, are made of plastic 100 times lighter than glass. The domes provide space for meetings and exhibitions and offer a stunning view of Rotterdam's skyline. But their primary purpose is to demonstrate the potential of floating architecture. By 2040, Rotterdam expects to have up to 1,200 homes floating in the harbor.[4]

Dredging removes sand from the bottom of the ocean and deposits it along the coast.

for approximately 20 years for half the cost. It is flexible and upkeep is easy—as the sea level rises, simply add more sand.

However, natural remedies such as the *zandmotor* may not always be enough. To meet the needs of flood-prone urban areas, engineers are developing high-tech dike improvements. These include new dike materials, such as flexible cement and special fabrics that decrease internal erosion and dike breaches. Biological engineers are also developing tougher breeds of grass that can absorb more wave energy. In some areas, nature and engineering will be combined by placing small

HOW TO TEST A DIKE

An international research team, including engineers from the United States, participated in Smart Dike testing in the Netherlands during 2012. For the test, the team embedded sensors in a full-sized dike that was built inside a specially constructed basin. They slowly added water to the basin, increasing pressure on the dike until it collapsed.

Sensors included shape-acceleration-pore pressure (SAPP) arrays, which measure soil deformation, vibration, and pore pressure at specific locations beneath and around the dike. These data are combined with GPS and satellite-based radar (InSAR) measurements, accurate to the millimeter, which show how much a dike has shifted or sunk due to aging or environmental stresses such as floods.

sand engines in front of existing dikes. The sand will absorb some of the waves' power, lessening the impact on aging dikes.

Though still in the testing stage, the Smart Dike is embedded with electronic sensors that give engineers and dike maintenance workers real-time information. This would allow workers to respond to problems before they are visible on the outside. Sensors measure water height, water pressure, moisture, and temperature. They send an alarm signal when the dike is at risk of breaching. By adding such technology to existing dikes, the Netherlands hopes to stop catastrophes before they happen.

LESSONS FOR NEW ORLEANS

Like much of the Netherlands, New Orleans lies below sea level. Many of its wetlands were dredged and filled to form new land. The land has since dried and sunk, but like the Netherlands, it remains dry because levees and pumping stations keep the Gulf of Mexico at bay. But Hurricane Katrina was a wake-up call. In 2005, it flooded 80 percent of the city, killing approximately 1,600 people and displacing approximately 200,000.[5] In retrospect, the devastation was not surprising. The New Orleans levees were built on outdated standards that greatly underestimated storm strengths. Even after the Army Corps of Engineers spent approximately $14 billion to upgrade the system after Hurricane Katrina, the city's system is still 100 times less safe than the system in the Netherlands, protecting against a 1-in-100-year flood rather than a 1-in-10,000-year flood.[6]

After Hurricane Katrina, many engineers suggested the United States follow the Netherlands' example. They wanted to surround New Orleans with dikes or build a barrier to block the sea from flooding the city during a storm. But, according to Dr. William Mitsch of Ohio State University, this would not only be prohibitively expensive; it would also ruin the estuary along the coast of Louisiana that supports the Gulf fishery. Instead, Mitsch and other experts favor ecological engineering. This would include wetlands restoration such as dredging and pumping coastal sediments to build up the land again. Other wetlands could be restored by opening some levees to restore original river flow. However, other engineers, including Robert Nicholls of the University of Southampton in the United Kingdom, caution hard defenses will still be necessary even after ecological ones are implemented.

Neighborhoods in New Orleans remained flooded two weeks after Hurricane Katrina hit on August 29, 2005.

SUCCESS IN NEW ORLEANS

After the storm surge from Hurricane Katrina breached levees and flooded New Orleans in 2005, the Dutch firm Arcadis helped design a two-mile (3.2 km) storm-surge barrier. The barrier protected the city from Hurricane Isaac in August 2012. The Lower Ninth Ward, devastated during Hurricane Katrina, was untouched by Hurricane Isaac. According to Arcadis executive Piet Dircke, "Isaac was a tremendous victory for New Orleans. All the barriers were closed; all the levees held; all the pumps worked. You didn't hear about it? No, because nothing happened."[8]

As coastal regions prepare for climate change, environmental engineers will be busy. They will be asked to design flood-control systems to withstand sea-level rise and stronger storm surges. They will design storm-resistant structures that can survive in these areas. To succeed in this endeavor, tomorrow's engineers might glean several lessons from the Netherlands' experience. First, plan for the long term—more than 100 years. Second, develop a comprehensive plan. Third, build smarter, not necessarily bigger. Fourth, work with nature, not against it. And the most important lesson, according to the Dutch: "vigilance . . . must be eternal."[7]

DR. WILLIAM MITSCH

Dr. William Mitsch's life's work has made him known around the world as a champion of wetlands and their restoration. He is one of the founders of the new study of ecological engineering.

Mitsch has degrees in mechanical engineering and environmental engineering sciences, as well as a PhD in systems ecology. He has worked in engineering and ecological systems departments at the Illinois Institute of Technology, the University of Louisville, and Ohio State University. In 2012, he moved to Florida Gulf Coast University to develop programs that will allow the Everglades and coastal wetlands to coexist safely with Gulf Coast development efforts.

One of Mitsch's major accomplishments is the Olentangy River Wetland Research Park on the campus of Ohio State University. Mitsch seeded one of the park's two 3-acre (1 ha) wetlands with 13 species of plants and left the other to grow on its own. He and his students have studied the wetlands throughout their development. Mitsch's philosophy is that "the best architect is nature itself."[9]

Mitsch's career has focused on wetland restoration.

CHAPTER 9

ENGINEERING THE FUTURE

The future of environmental engineering is broad and varied. People concerned about the environment in general, or about any specific aspect of the environment, may consider joining this field. Many times environmental engineers are asked to design systems that function with the environment, thereby preventing environmental damage. But often the job will involve developing plans to clean up after a disaster or restoring an ecosystem that was badly damaged or destroyed.

Engineers can prevent environmental damage by using reservoirs that safely hold industrial waste.

RESTORING A MINED ECOSYSTEM

The Tri-State Mining District comprises a region of more than 2,500 square miles (6,475 sq km), where the states of Kansas, Oklahoma, and Missouri meet.[1] From the 1890s to the early 1970s, 2 million short tons (1.8 million metric tons) of lead and 9 million short tons (8.1 million metric tons) of zinc were mined from this region.[2] After mining ceased and water was no longer pumped from the mines, the liquid built up in mine cavities and mixed with heavy metal waste. As water levels rose in the mines, water began flowing out of them. By 1979, acid mine water containing high concentrations of heavy metals such as lead, zinc, iron, cadmium, manganese, and arsenic was flowing into nearby Tar Creek and its tributaries.

In 1983, the US Environmental Protection Agency (EPA) listed the Tar Creek area as a Superfund site, giving it the highest toxicity rating in the country. The EPA created the Superfund program in 1980 to clean up abandoned hazardous waste sites around the country. In 2008, Dr. Robert Nairn, ecological engineer in the School of Civil Engineering and Environmental Science at the University of Oklahoma, and his research group began a project to purify the mine water using an ecologically engineered passive treatment process.

The treatment system consists of ten ponds, including four sets of parallel ponds. As water travels by gravity through the pairs of ponds, various chemical and biological processes remove heavy metals. Then clean, clear water leaves the last pond to reenter Tar Creek.

Dr. Nairn leads students through an environmental project at heavily polluted Tar Creek.

When acid mine water enters Pond 1, it appears very red due to iron oxidation, commonly called rust. Pond 1 targets iron. Solid iron particles settle to the bottom of the pond, removing them from the water. Oxidation removes some iron compounds. Water then enters Ponds 2N (for north) and 2S (for south), where settling removes additional iron. Rooted water plants slow water flow through these ponds. Ponds 3N and 3S target lead, zinc, and cadmium. Bacterial reactions remove zinc and sulfate from the water. In Ponds 4N and 4S, a small windmill and a solar panel run air compressors that produce air bubbles to add oxygen to the water. Ponds 5N and 5S are horizontal-flow limestone beds. The limestone decreases the water's acidity as it combines with zinc and manganese. In the final pond, remaining solids are removed from the now clear water. Plants add oxygen. This system of treatment ponds purifies approximately one-fifth of the total acid mine water outflow from the mines in the Tar Creek watershed.[3]

RESTORING BROWNFIELD SITES

The EPA Brownfields Program transforms brownfields, generally products of former industrial or commercial activities, into safe, functional land, such as natural or recreational areas or commercial centers. Government agencies and private groups or industries cooperate on these projects.

In ideal cases, the cleanups train people for new environmental careers and improve the community's quality of life.

In 2005, a company called Mother Earth purchased a 34-acre (13.8 ha) Studebaker vehicle plant in South Bend, Indiana. The company planned to use the site for a recycling plant. The old plant was deconstructed for reuse. Many recovered materials were used in the construction of the new Green Tech Recycling facility. Other recovered materials were sold for reuse or donated locally. An estimated 99 percent of the material from the Studebaker plant was recovered and reused.[4]

Many contaminated or abandoned brownfield sites in the United States have been revitalized through cleanup and repurposing. All of these required the expertise of environmental engineers or others with environmental or ecological training.

DECONSTRUCTING A STUDEBAKER PLANT

Deconstruction of the Studebaker plant in South Bend, Indiana, resulted in the recovery and reuse of 99 percent of its materials, including:

- 15,000 short tons (13,608 metric tons) of concrete and bricks (reused on-site or sold for reuse)
- 5,000 cubic yards (3,823 cu m) of wood (mulched, donated for landscaping, or sold for reuse)
- signage (reused for a local baseball field)
- gate (reused for baseball field disabled parking)[5]

ELECTRONIC WASTE CLEANUP

A different type of environmental problem is how to recycle the massive amounts of electronic waste generated by the world's wealthy nations. An international report published in December 2013 by the StEP (Solving the E-Waste Problem) Initiative predicts that, by 2017, the amount of discarded electronic waste, or e-waste, produced around the world will increase by 33 percent.[6] The United States generates approximately 66 pounds (30 kg) of e-waste per person per year, and six other countries generate even more. In 2010, the United States produced approximately 258.2 million units of used electronics, including computers, monitors, televisions, and cell phones.[7] Of these, 171.4 million were collected for recycling and 14.4 million were exported for reuse in other countries.[8]

E-waste presents two opportunities for environmental engineers. First, recycling recovers and reuses the precious nonrenewable resources found in electronics, especially metals such as copper, gold, silver, and palladium. The recycling industry in the United States is growing. According to E-Stewards, an organization that certifies electronics recycling programs, full-time jobs in electronics recycling increased from 6,000 in 2002 to 45,000 in 2011.[9] New technologies exist for this fledgling industry, but more are needed. Second, the circuit boards, wiring, and electric connections in electronic devices are filled with toxic materials, including heavy metals that can be recycled, plus flame retardants and other chemicals. These substances are dangerous when burned or when they leak into landfills and pollute soil and groundwater. For an environmental engineer, these problems may be solved by designing better landfills to prevent leakage or waste, developing methods to mine landfills for the recyclable materials they contain, or implementing methods to collect and recycle electronics instead of disposing of them.

Many parts of electronic devices can be recycled, including the metal.

CLIMATE ENGINEERING: GOOD OR BAD?

While most engineers advocate for adaptations or mitigations to climate change, such as protecting coastlines and lowering the release of greenhouse gases into the atmosphere, some geoengineers want to change the climate. Some geoengineers look into ways to remove carbon dioxide from the atmosphere and store it elsewhere by planting trees or developing machines to suck out carbon dioxide from the atmosphere. But many people believe changing something as huge and important as climate, with no understanding of the consequences, would be risky.

LOOKING FORWARD

What is the future of environmental engineering? According to the book *200 Best Jobs for Renewing America*, the outlook is bright. An increased need for green technology in the coming decades will spur environmental engineering job growth. Companies must comply with environmental regulations. New methods will be needed to clean up and prevent environmental hazards. Population growth will require more public health solutions. Experts in waste treatment and disposal will be in demand. Those with expertise in computer modeling can find jobs predicting future environmental impacts and developing cleanup projects.

Finally, climate change opens up a whole range of challenges for environmental engineers. Climate change causes water shortages

CONCEPTS OF ECOLOGICAL ENGINEERING

Dr. Mitsch identifies five key concepts that help define the emerging field of ecological engineering:

- Nature contributes as much or more to ecosystem design as does the human designer.

- A failed ecosystem restoration can increase our understanding of ecological theory and function.

- The engineer must consider the ecosystem as a whole.

- Ecosystem services, including natural energy sources such as solar, wind, and hydrologic energy, are the foundation of all designs.

- Natural ecosystems should never be disturbed or eliminated unless absolutely necessary.

and puts stress on agricultural systems. It also contributes to severe storms that flood places such as the Netherlands and New Orleans. Environmental engineer Dennis P. Lettenmaier believes one challenge will be to adapt information from global climate models to meet the needs of smaller communities. For example, what effect will changes in precipitation have on the movement of water in a single watershed? Many climate change problems must be solved on a local or regional scale—and environmental engineers will be the ones to solve them.

HANDS-ON PROJECT
CREATE A WATER FILTER

Water from lakes, streams, and rivers may contain harmful substances that make it unsafe to drink. It is necessary to filter and purify water to remove these substances and make it potable. You can create a water filter using things you can find in your home and local grocery and home stores.

You'll need:

1.5 gallons (5 L) of water	1 large measuring cup or bowl
2.5 cups (0.5 L) of dirt	1 cup (0.25 L) small pebbles
2 2-liter soft drink bottles with caps	1.5 cups (0.35 L) multipurpose sand
1 coffee filter	1.5 cups (0.35 L) play or beach sand
1 rubber band	

Pour 0.5 gallons (2 L) of water and the dirt into one of the soft drink bottles. Cap the bottle and shake it to make dirty water. Note how the water looks and smells. Let the dirty water settle as you construct the filter.

To make the filter, take the remaining soft drink bottle and cut the bottom off it. Remove the cap and attach the coffee filter securely to the top of the bottle with the rubber band. Place the bottle upside down in the large measuring cup or bowl.

Carefully pour the small pebbles into the bottle. The coffee filter should keep them from spilling out of the bottle. Then, pour the multipurpose sand over the pebbles. Pour the play or beach sand over the multipurpose sand.

It is important to clean your filter before you use it. Carefully pour 0.75 gallons (3 L) clean tap water through the filter. Do not disturb the top layer of sand as you pour.

Now you are ready to filter the dirty water. Slowly pour two-thirds of the water over the sand and through the filter. Do not disturb the sediment that has settled at the bottom of the dirty water bottle.

Compare the remaining dirty water to the filtered water in the measuring cup or beaker. Has its appearance or smell changed?

Your filtered water is still not safe to drink. There may still be substances and organisms in it that make it unsafe. If you are thirsty, take a drink from your home's tap instead.

PLANNING A CAREER

Future environmental engineers should take high school courses in science (including chemistry, biology, and physics) and math (including algebra, trigonometry, and calculus).

↓

Environmental engineers must have a bachelor's degree in engineering. The degree can be in environmental engineering or in another engineering field. Some universities have five-year programs that allow students to obtain both bachelor's and master's degrees.

↓

To become licensed, environmental engineering graduates should receive passing scores on the Fundamentals of Engineering exam and on the Professional Engineering exam. An engineer can become board certified through the American Academy of Environmental Engineers and Scientists.

ESSENTIAL FACTS
DEEPWATER HORIZON OIL SPILL

PROJECT DATES

The *Deepwater Horizon* oil rig exploded on April 20, 2010. It took BP 86 days, until July 15, to shut off the flow of oil. Cleanup on the water continued throughout the summer and fall. BP and the US Coast Guard officially discontinued coastal cleanup in June 2013, but oil continues to wash up.

KEY PLAYERS

BP was nominally in charge of cleanup, but many US government agencies also participated, as did environmental departments and oil spill task forces from affected coastal states. Thousands of individuals, agencies, and companies around the country volunteered their services and equipment.

KEY TOOLS AND TECHNOLOGIES

- Booms and skimmers control and remove oil from the water's surface.

- Controlled burns and chemical dispersants removed and dispersed oil from the water.

THE IMPACT OF THE *DEEPWATER HORIZON* OIL SPILL

The spill highlighted inadequacies in plans to prevent and clean up a massive spill. It showed that the technologies used, particularly booms and dispersants, are imperfect. The spill spurred research to improve these technologies.

ESSENTIAL FACTS
WATER SCARCITY IN AFRICA

PROJECT DATES
In 2002, the UN Environment Programme listed "freshwater depletion and degradation" as an "existing and emerging" environmental issue. In 2012, the National Academy of Engineering listed access to clean water as one of the "grand challenges for engineering." The problem is ongoing.

KEY PLAYERS
No single individual or group is tackling this problem. Small-scale projects are underway in various parts of Africa. Scientist Laura Brunson is developing filters to purify water in Ethiopia. Ariane Kirtley and her organization Amman Imman build boreholes to supply desert communities.

KEY TOOLS AND TECHNOLOGIES
- Wells are bored into underground aquifers.

- Water is piped from rivers or springs and purified for use. Often, purification techniques are specific to an area or even an individual.

THE IMPACT OF WATER SCARCITY IN AFRICA
UN programs have made good progress in some areas. For example, access to clean water in Uganda has improved. Individuals and university engineering groups have developed promising programs and technologies. However, much remains to be done.

ESSENTIAL FACTS
THE NETHERLANDS' DIKES

PROJECT DATES

The Netherlands has been building dikes to hold back the North Sea for more than 2,000 years. The latest major project was the Delta Works, completed in 1997. Today, the Netherlands is implementing more ecologically sound protection methods.

KEY PLAYERS

Many engineers and workers over many years are responsible for the Netherlands' flood-control system.

KEY TOOLS AND TECHNOLOGIES

- Dikes with electronic sensors detect threats of flooding and close off saltwater bays and estuaries.

- The *zandmotor* protects the Dutch coastline by allowing waves and tides to move sand barriers, and dikes.

THE IMPACT OF THE NETHERLANDS' DIKES

The Netherlands' efforts have taught engineers much about designing structures to withstand great water pressures. They are now learning more about working with nature rather than against it. They are sharing their engineering expertise with the United States and other nations with coastal regions at risk from rising sea levels.

GLOSSARY

adsorption
The sticking of molecules to the surface of a solid substance.

aquifer
An underground, water-holding layer of sand, gravel, or rock; the storage area for groundwater.

borehole
A closed, narrow shaft that reaches deep down to the clean, permanent aquifer underlying the region.

breakwater
An offshore structure that protects dikes, harbors, and beaches from the force of waves.

brownfield
A piece of property that contains hazardous materials or chemicals.

controlled burn
An oil-spill cleanup technique in which oil is corralled by means of a boom and then set on fire.

emulsion
A mixture of tiny droplets of oil and water that forms a relatively stable mixture.

estuary
The area where a river flows into the sea or ocean.

infrastructure
Physical and organizational structures required for smooth operation of a society; for example, roads, buildings, power plants, and water systems.

nanoparticle

A very tiny microscopic particle.

oil slick

A thin sheet of oil on the surface of water.

oxidation

A chemical reaction involving oxygen.

permeable

A substance that allows liquids or gases to pass through it.

potable

Water that is free from contamination and safe to drink.

watershed

All of the land area where the underground water underneath it drains into a particular body of water, such as a large river, lake, or the ocean.

ADDITIONAL RESOURCES

SELECTED BIBLIOGRAPHY

"Delta Works Flood Protection, Rhine-Meuse-Scheldt Delta, Netherlands." *Water-technology.net*. Net Resources International, 2012. Web. 2 Jan. 2014.

Fingas, Merv. *The Basics of Oil Spill Cleanup*, 3rd ed. Boca Raton, FL: CRC, 2013. Print.

"How Amman Imman: Water is Life Began." *Amman Imman Water Is Life*. Amman Imman. 2005-2013. Web. 28 Dec. 2013.

Mihelcic, James R., Ph.D., Lauren M. Fry, Elizabeth A. Myre, Linda D. Phillips, P.E., and Brian D. Barkdoll, Ph.D., P.E. *Field Guide to Environmental Engineering for Development Workers: Water, Sanitation, and Indoor Air*. Reston, VA: ASCE, 2009. Print.

FURTHER READINGS

Farrell, Courtney. *The Gulf of Mexico Oil Spill*. Edina, MN: ABDO, 2011. Print.

Hoeksema, Robert J. *Designed for Dry Feet: Flood Protection and Land Reclamation in the Netherlands*. Reston, VA: American Society of Civil Engineers, 2006. Print.

Langwith, Jacqueline, ed. *Water*. Detroit: Greenhaven, 2010. Print.

Maczulak, Anne E. *Environmental Engineering: Designing a Sustainable Future*. New York: Facts on File, 2010. Print.

WEBSITES

To learn more about Great Achievements in Engineering, visit **booklinks.abdopublishing.com**. These links are routinely monitored and updated to provide the most current information available.

FOR MORE INFORMATION

For more information on this subject, contact or visit the following organizations:

Department of Civil & Environmental Engineering

Jerry Yang & Akiko Yamazaki Environment & Energy Building

Stanford University

473 Via Ortega, Room 314, MC 4020

Stanford, CA 94305

650-723-3074

http://cee.standford.edu

Tour the facilities of one of the country's best environmental engineering departments.

Hurricane Katrina Tour, Gray Line Tours New Orleans

600 Decatur Street, Suite 308

New Orleans, LA 70130

800-233-2628

http://www.graylineneworleans.com

This tour shows a breached levee and areas that were destroyed. Tour goers learn how coastal wetlands, levees, and severe weather are connected.

SOURCE NOTES

CHAPTER 1. A SPILL IN THE GULF

1. Antonia Juhasz. *Black Tide: The Devastating Impact of the Gulf Oil Spill.* Hoboken, NJ: Wiley, 2011. Print. 5–8.

2. Ibid. 85.

3. Russell McLendon. "BP's Oiled Animals: Where Are They Now?" *Mother Nature Network.* MNN Holdings, 16 Apr. 2013. Web. 19 Dec. 2013.

4. "Environmental Engineers." *Occupational Outlook Handbook.* US Bureau of Labor Statistics, 8 Jan. 2014. Web. 13 Dec. 2013.

CHAPTER 2. ENVIRONMENTAL ENGINEERING

None.

CHAPTER 3. THE *DEEPWATER* CLEANUP

1. "Oil Pollution of Marine Habitats." *WOR 1.* World Ocean Review, 2010. Web. 19 Dec. 2013.

2. Cutler J. Cleveland. "Deepwater Horizon Oil Spill." *The Encyclopedia of Earth.* Environmental Information Coalition, 22 Feb. 2013. Web. 13 Dec. 2013.

3. Reuters. "Timeline of the Gulf of Mexico Oil Spill." *CNBC.* CNBC, 30 July 2010. Web. 13 Dec. 2013.

4. Cutler J. Cleveland. "Deepwater Horizon Oil Spill." *The Encyclopedia of Earth.* Environmental Information Coalition, 22 Feb. 2013. Web. 13 Dec. 2013.

5. Jeremy Repanich. "The Deepwater Horizon Spill by the Numbers." *Popular Mechanics.* Hearst Communications, 10 Aug. 2010. Web. 13 Dec. 2013.

6. "History's Worst Oil Spills." *History.* A&E Television Networks, n.d. Web. 13 Dec. 2013.

7. Antonia Juhasz. *Black Tide: The Devastating Impact of the Gulf Oil Spill.* Hoboken, NJ: Wiley, 2011. Print. 85.

8. Cutler J. Cleveland. "Deepwater Horizon Oil Spill." *The Encyclopedia of Earth.* Environmental Information Coalition, 22 Feb. 2013. Web. 13 Dec. 2013.

9. Jeremy Repanich. "The Deepwater Horizon Spill by the Numbers." *Popular Mechanics.* Hearst Communications, 10 Aug. 2010. Web. 13 Dec. 2013.

10. Ibid.

11. "Spill Containment Methods." *NOAA Office of Response and Restoration.* NOAA, 20 Feb. 2014. Web. 14 Dec. 2013.

12. Jeremy Repanich. "The Deepwater Horizon Spill by the Numbers." *Popular Mechanics.* Hearst Communications, 10 Aug. 2010. Web. 13 Dec. 2013.

13. Ibid.

14. Merv Fingas. *The Basics of Oil Spill Cleanup.* 3rd ed. Boca Raton, FL: CRC, 2013. Print. 42.

15. Jeremy Repanich. "The Deepwater Horizon Spill by the Numbers." *Popular Mechanics.* Hearst Communications, 10 Aug. 2010. Web. 13 Dec. 2013.

16. Cutler J. Cleveland. "Deepwater Horizon Oil Spill." *The Encyclopedia of Earth.* Environmental Information Coalition, 22 Feb. 2013. Web. 13 Dec. 2013.

CHAPTER 4. FUTURE CLEANUPS

1. Jessica Hartogs. "Three Years after BP Oil Spill, Active Clean-Up Ends in Three States." *CBS News*. CBS Interactive, 10 June 2013. Web. 15 Dec. 2013.

2. Debbie Elliott. "For BP Cleanup, 2013 Meant 4.6 Million Pounds of Oily Gunk." *NPR*. NPR, 21 Dec. 2013. Web. 21 Dec. 2013.

3. Matt Smith. "Empty Nets in Louisiana Three Years after the Spill." *CNN U.S.* Cable News Network, 29 Apr. 2013. Web. 15 Dec. 2013.

4. Adam Gabbatt. "BP Oil Spill: Kevin Costner's Oil-Water Separation Machines Help with Clean-Up." *The Guardian*. Guardian News and Media Limited, 16 June 2010. Web. 13 Dec. 2013.

5. Mark Schrope. "Researchers Debate Oil-Spill Remedy." *Nature*. Nature Publishing Group, 22 Jan. 2013. Web. 23 Dec. 2013.

6. "BP Oil Spill Cleanup Toxic to Key Species." *CBC News*. CBC, 30 Nov. 2012. Web. 13 Dec 2013.

7. Carly Gillis. "New Oil Spill Technology Cleans Four Times Faster than Industry Standard." *CounterSpill*. Counterspill, 20 Oct. 2011. Web. 26 Dec. 2013.

CHAPTER 5. OVERCOMING WATER SCARCITY

1 "Fatoumata's Story." *WaterAid*. WaterAid, n.d. Web. 28 Dec. 2013.

2. "Water and Women." *Voss Foundation*. Voss Foundation, 2014. Web. 28 Dec. 2013.

3. Jessica Prois and Eleanor Goldberg. "World Water Day 2013: How Shortages Affect Women, Kids, Hunger (And What You Can Do)." *Huff Post Water*. Huffington Post, 22 Mar. 2013. Web. 27 Dec. 2013.

4. "Provide Access to Clean Water." *NAE Grand Challenges for Engineering*. National Academy of Sciences, n.d. Web. 16 Dec. 2013.

5. Ibid.

6. "Provide Access to Clean Water." *NAE Grand Challenges for Engineering*. National Academy of Sciences, n.d. Web. 16 Dec. 2013.

7. "UN Entities Say Post-2015 Development Agenda Must Address Inequity in Access to Clean Water, Sanitation." *UN News Centre*. UN News Centre, 30 Oct. 2013. Web. 20 Feb. 2014.

8. "Water Scarcity." *UN Water*. UN-Water, 2013. Web. 20 Feb. 2014.

9. "Water Scarcity." *International Decade for Action 'Water for Life' 2005–2015*. UN Department of Economic and Social Affairs, 21 Feb. 2014. Web. 21 Feb. 2014.

10. "Water Scarcity." *UN Water*. UN-Water, 2013. Web. 20 Feb. 2014.

11. "Sanitation." UN Water. UN-Water, 2013. Web. 20 Feb. 2014.

12. James R. Mihelcic, et al. *Field Guide to Environmental Engineering for Development Workers. Water, Sanitation, and Indoor Air*. Reston, VA: ASCE, 2009. Print. 161, 165–168.

13. Ibid. 16–19.

14. Jessica Prois and Eleanor Goldberg. "World Water Day 2013: How Shortages Affect Women, Kids, Hunger (And What You Can Do)." *Huff Post Water*. Huffington Post, 22 Mar. 2013. Web. 27 Dec. 2013.

SOURCE NOTES CONTINUED

15. Katherine Sentlinger. "Water Scarcity and Agriculture." *Water Project*. Water Project, n.d. Web. 27 Dec. 2013.

16. Maryruth Belsey Priebe. "Social Entrepreneurs Create Two Amazingly Simple Water Carriers." *Noble Profit*. Creative Entity, 2011. Web. 28 Dec. 2013.

17. Nicole Itano. "In Rural South Africa, 'Hippos' Carry Load." *Christian Science Monitor*. Christian Science Monitor, 5 Apr. 2002. Web. 28 Dec. 2013.

18. Calestous Juma. "Poor Infrastructure Is Africa's Soft Underbelly." *Forbes*. Forbes.com, 25 Oct. 2012. Web. 28 Dec. 2013.

19. "Mission and Vision." *Amman Imman Water Is Life*. Amman Imman, n.d. Web. 28 Dec. 2013.

20. Kyle Stevenson. "Half of Limpopo Live in Poverty." *Local News*. SA Breaking News, 18 Sept. 2013. Web. 29 Dec. 2013.

21. Eric Harshfeld, et al. "Water Purification in Rural South Africa: Ethical Analysis and Reflections on Collaborative Community Engagement Projects in Engineering." *Int. J. Service Learning in Engineering* 4.1 (Spring 2009): 1–14. Print.

CHAPTER 6. ENGINEERING SUCCESSES

1. "How Amman Imman: Water is Life Began." *Amman Imman Water Is Life*. Amman Imman, n.d. Web. 28 Dec. 2013.

2. "Mission and Vision." *Amman Imman Water Is Life*. Amman Imman, n.d. Web. 28 Dec. 2013.

3. "Our Borehole Villages Photo Galleries." *Amman Imman Water Is Life*. Amman Imman, n.d. Web. 30 Dec. 2013.

4. "Gravity Water." *SunStove Organization*. SunStove Organization, 2011. Web. 9 Nov. 2013.

5. "How Biosand Water Filtration Systems Work." *Water Project*. Water Project, n.d. Web. 1 Jan. 2014.

6. "Projects: Zambia." *Biosand Filters.info*. Centre for Affordable Water and Sanitation Technology, n.d. Web. 20 Feb. 2014.

7. "Projects: Kenya." *Biosand Filters.info*. Centre for Affordable Water and Sanitation Technology, n.d. Web. 20 Feb. 2014.

8. Caroline Perry. "Engineering a Better Life." *Harvard Gazette*. Harvard School of Engineering and Applied Sciences, 31 Oct. 2013. Web. 1 Nov. 2013.

CHAPTER 7. HOLDING BACK THE SEA

1. "Europe: Netherlands." *World Factbook*. CIA, 2013. Web. 1 Jan. 2014.

2. Matt Rosenberg. "Polders and Dikes of the Netherlands." *About.com Geography*. About.com, n.d. Web. 11 Dec. 2013.

3. "Sea Dikes." *Ecomare Encyclopedia*. Ecomare, n.d. Web. 12 Dec. 2013.

4. "Dike Technology." *Delft University of Technology*, n.d. Web. 2 Jan. 2014.

5. Lee Krystek. "The Zuiderzee and Delta Works of the Netherlands." *Seven Wonders of the Modern World*. Museum of Unnatural History, 2011. Web. 2 Jan. 2014.

6. "Delta Works Flood Protection, Rhine-Meuse-Scheldt Delta, Netherlands." *Water-technology.net*. Net Resources International, 2012. Web. 2 Jan. 2014.

7. Ibid.

8. Andrew Higgins. "Lessons for U.S. from a Flood-Prone Land." *New York Times*. New York Times, 14 Nov. 2012. Web. 9 Nov. 2013.

9. "Coastal Flood Risk The Netherlands." *Netherlands*. Climate Adaptation.eu, n.d. Web. 16 Dec. 2013.

CHAPTER 8. GEARING UP FOR CLIMATE CHANGE

1. Mason Inman. "Working with Water." *Nature Reports Climate Change*. Nature Publishing Group, 6 Apr. 2010. Web. 16 Dec. 2013.

2. John McQuaid. "Dutch System of Flood Control an Engineering Marvel." *New Orleans Times-Picayune*. NOLA Media Group, 13 Nov. 2005. Web. 9 Nov. 2013.

3. Cheryl Katz. "To Control Floods, the Dutch Turn to Nature for Inspiration." *Environment360*. Yale University, 21 Feb. 2013. Web. 9 Nov. 2013.

4. Tim Folger. "Rising Seas." *National Geographic Magazine*. National Geographic Society, Sept. 2013. Web. 3 Jan. 2014.

5. Marshall Brain and Robert Lamb. "What Is a Levee?" *How Stuff Works*. How Stuff Works, n.d. Web. 11 Dec. 2013.

6. Ibid.

7. John McQuaid. "Dutch System of Flood Control an Engineering Marvel." *New Orleans Times-Picayune*. NOLA Media Group, 13 Nov. 2005. Web. 9 Nov. 2013.

8. Tim Folger. "Rising Seas." *National Geographic Magazine*. National Geographic Society, Sept. 2013. Web. 3 Jan. 2014.

9. Spencer Hunt. "Biologist Bill Mitsch Spent Career at Ohio State Creating World-Class Wetlands." *Columbus Dispatch*. Dispatch Printing Company, 30 Sept. 2012. Web. 20 Feb. 2014.

CHAPTER 9. ENGINEERING THE FUTURE

1. "Tar Creek Superfund Site Tri-State Mining District—Chat Mining Waste." *United States Environmental Protection Agency*. US EPA, June 2007. Web. 5 Jan. 2014.

2. R. W. Nairn, et al. "A Large, Multi-Cell Ecologically Engineered Passive Treatment System for Ferruginous Lead-Zinc Mine Waste." *Mine Water and Innovative Thinking*. Sydney, NS: International Mine Water Association, 2010. Print. 21.

3. Ibid. 21–22.

4. "Value-Added Deconstruction in South Bend, IN Generates a $1.4 Million Revenue Stream." *U.S. Environmental Protection Agency*. US EPA, Jan. 2009. Web. 5 Jan. 2014.

5. Ibid.

6. Tanya Lewis. "World's E-Waste to Grow 33% by 2017, Says Global Report." *LiveScience*. TechMedia Network, 15 Dec. 2013. Web. 20 Feb. 2014.

7. Ibid.

8. Ibid.

9. Adam Minter. "U.S. Isn't Flooding the Third World with E-Waste." *Bloomberg Opinion*. Bloomberg, 26 May 2013. Web. 5 Jan. 2014.

INDEX

ABOUT THE AUTHOR

Carol Hand has a PhD in zoology with a specialization in marine ecology and a special interest in environmental science. Before becoming a science writer, she taught college, wrote for standardized testing companies, and developed multimedia science curricula. She has written approximately 20 books for young people on topics ranging from glaciers to genetics to fusion energy.

ABOUT THE CONTENT CONSULTANT

James H. Clarke is professor of the Practice of Civil & Environmental Engineering, professor of Earth & Environmental Sciences, and director of Graduate Studies for graduate degree options in environmental engineering, environmental science, and environmental management at Vanderbilt University. His research interests include risk-informed regulation, investigation, remediation, and long-term management of legacy chemical and radioactive waste sites and the environmental impacts of conventional and emerging energy technologies.